BEASTIES IN MY BACKYARD

Written by Camilla de la Bédoyère

Edited and Designed by Calcium Creative

Publisher: Zeta Jones

Associate Publisher: Maxime Boucknooghe

Editorial Director: Laura Knowles

Art Director: Susi Martin

ISBN 978-0-545-91749-0

10 9 8 7 6 5 4 3 2 1   15 16 17 18 19

Printed and bound in China
First Scholastic edition, October 2015

BEASTIES IN MY BACKYARD

CONTENTS

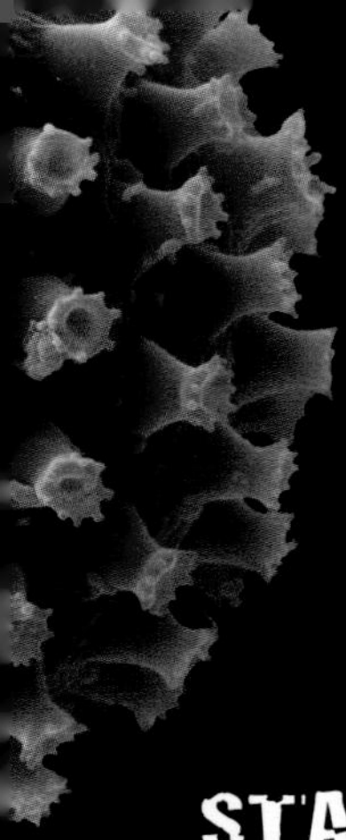

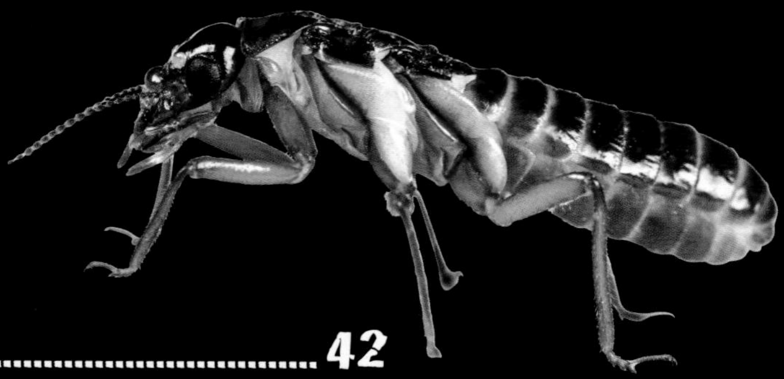

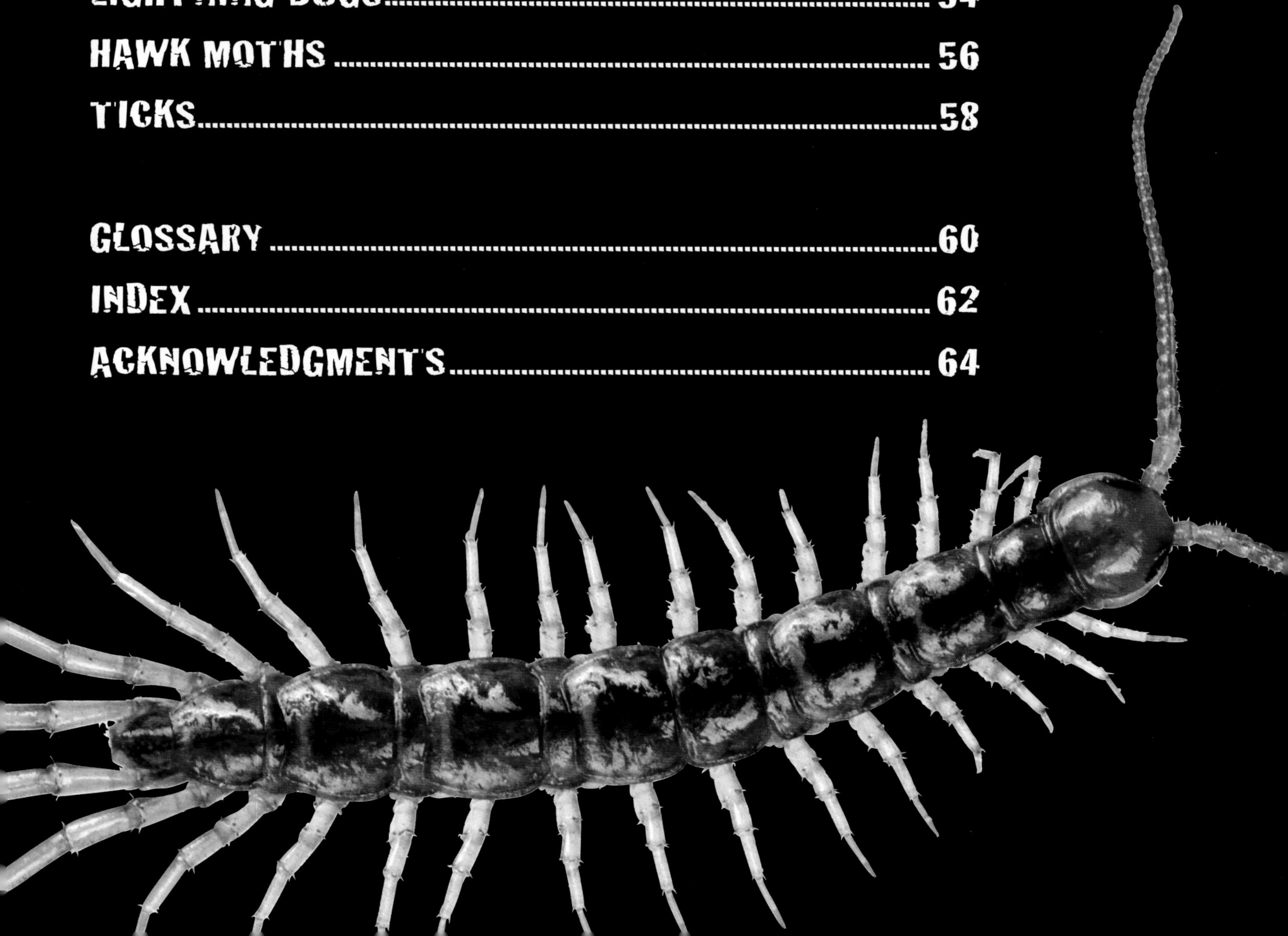

BEAST'S BENEATH YOUR FEET

Backyards are packed with life. Stand still and use your eyes and ears to discover some of the many animals that make their homes in backyards, parks, gardens, and wasteland. The most fascinating of these creatures are the **invertebrates**—small animals that do not have backbones.

HABITATS ARE HOMES

Habitats are places where animals or plants live. A backyard is a habitat, but so is the soil inside a plant pot, a **compost** bin, or the cracks in a tree's bark. A garden is packed with these "microhabitats."

*Many adult insects have **compound eyes** made up of lots of tiny lenses. They are so big, the bug can see all around.*

Exoskeleton
Invertebrates do not have bones to support their bodies, which is why they cannot grow very big. Many of them have a tough skin, called an exoskeleton, instead. Exoskeletons can be colorful and patterned.

⊕ LIFE CYCLES

The story of how an animal grows from an egg into an adult that lays eggs is called a life cycle. Young **insects** are called **larvae** or **nymphs**. Many look very different from the adults they will become.

Body parts
*Invertebrate bodies are divided into sections, or parts. Insects have three sections: a head, a **thorax**, and an **abdomen**.*

Sense organs
*Invertebrates use their senses to find out about the world. Like humans, they can see, smell, touch, taste, and hear, but some of their senses are far better than ours. The sensitive feelers on their heads are called **antennae**.*

Legs
Most invertebrates have legs. Insects have three pairs of legs, and spiders have four pairs of legs.

The invertebrates you are most likely to find in the backyard will be:
- **Arachnids** (spiders, mites, ticks, and scorpions)
- Insects (flies, butterflies, bees, beetles, and ants)
- Molluscs and annelids (slugs and snails, and worms)
- Centipedes, millipedes, and woodlice

WATER BEARS

Water bears are so small that most people do not even know they exist. These invertebrates belong to a group of about 1,000 species of animal called tardigrades. They are among the toughest and smallest creatures alive. Water bears have been on the planet for about 500 million years.

TOUGH BEASTS

Water bears prefer to live in damp or wet places. They can squeeze between particles of sand or soil in a backyard, and they can also survive in rivers and oceans. They can live in extreme conditions. They have been found in deserts and even in the soil under ice.

CLAWS

A water bear's feet are equipped with sharp, curved claws. The animal uses its claws to dig itself into a safe, damp habitat, such as moss or soil.

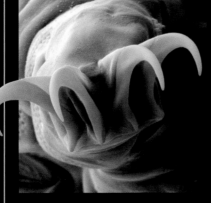

Hooked claws, seen using a powerful microscope.

Legs
Water bears have four pairs of short legs. They are used for crawling, walking, and swimming.

Repair
Scientists do not know how tardigrades survive extreme heat and cold, but they know that their bodies can quickly repair any damage.

SURVIVOR

When a tardigrade is caught in freezing temperatures or a drought, it can lose around 97 percent of the water in its body. When this happens, some species produce a sugar to protect their cell walls from damage.

SPACE BEARS

Water bears and other microscopic organisms were sent into space to test their survival in extreme conditions. In space, the water bears dehydrated, but they were rehydrated when they returned to Earth. Some of those that returned to Earth laid eggs.

This water bear's egg was laid in damp moss.

Piglike
Water bears are also known as moss piglets because they often live in moss and they look a bit like little pigs!

FACT FILE

TYPE
Class: Phylum
Order: Tardigrada

DIET
Plants and small animals

FOUND
Worldwide, including land, sea, and freshwater

0 ⁸/1,000 inch (2 mm)

SIZE • ¹/100–⁴/100 INCH (0.3–1.2 MM)

Stylets
Instead of teeth, water bears have hard, sharp stylets, which can pierce plant cells and small animals.

Tun
A water bear can survive some extreme conditions by turning itself into a "tun." It pulls its head and claws into its body, and it dries out

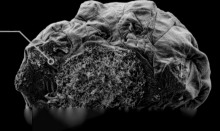

LIVING IN EXTREMES

Water bears can survive briefly in temperatures as hot as 257 °F (125 °C) and as cold as -458 °F (-272 °C)

GARDEN SNAILS

The common garden snail is a type of land snail. Most members of the snail's family—the mollusks—live in water. Garden snails are often seen as pests because they eat healthy plants. A large garden snail can leave a beautiful plant in shreds after just one night of feasting.

ON THE MOVE

When a snail moves, the muscles in its foot contract in waves, and it slides over the ground. Snails move out of their hiding places in the cool evenings and at night. During the day, they hide under rocks or leaves. In winter, garden snails **hibernate** to avoid freezing in the cold weather.

Shell
The snail's body makes its colorful shell for protection. The snail cannot separate itself from its shell because the shell is like hard skin.

SLIME

As the mollusk slithers forward, it leaves a telltale trail of mucus, or slime. The slime helps the snail or slug to move smoothly across plants, rocks, and other backyard obstacles. The mucus is produced by a gland in the mollusk's foot and varies depending on the season and what the snail has eaten.

Slime *helps a snail to move and to stick to surfaces.*

WIDESPREAD

This species of land snail is originally from Europe, but over time it has spread to parts of Asia, North America, and Africa. Garden snails are edible, which means that humans can safely eat them. In some countries, the snails are farmed for food or for their slime, which is sometimes used in cosmetics.

Slugs and snails may be pests in a garden, but they are important food for other visitors, such as birds, frogs, newts, toads, and lizards.

SLUGS

Slugs are closely related to snails, but they do not grow a protective shell. Slugs are rarely seen in the daytime because they dry out quickly in the sunshine. At night, they come out to eat backyard plants.

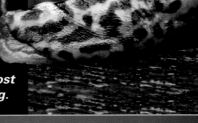

Leopard slugs grow to almost 5 inches (12 centimeters) long.

Tentacles
The head has two pairs of tentacles. An eye is on the tip of each of the two largest tentacles.

Moist skin
The skin is protected from sharp stones and from drying out by a thick mucus.

Foot
The muscular part of a mollusk's body is called its foot. The mollusk uses it to move.

FACT FILE

TYPE
Class: Gastropoda
Order: Pulmonata

DIET
Plants

FOUND
Worldwide, in damp or cool habitats

0   About ¾ inch (2 cm)

SIZE • ABOUT ¾ INCH–1½ INCHES (2–4 CM) (SHELL WIDTH)

CENTIPEDES

The name "centipede" means "100 feet." These common invertebrates can run very fast, but they do not really have that many feet. Centipedes, unlike millipedes, hunt other animals to eat. They use venomous (poisonous) claws to sting their **prey**, but they are mostly harmless to humans.

FACT FILE

TYPE
Class: Chilopoda
Order: Lithobiomorpha

DIET
Insects and spiders

FOUND
*Worldwide in cool,
damp places*

0   1²/₁₀ inches (30 mm)

**SIZE • ABOUT 1 INCH-
1¹/₃ INCHES (24–35 MM)**

Segments
*Centipedes are **arthropods**,
with a tough exoskeleton and
a body divided into segments.
The body is long, thin, and
slightly flattened.*

GROWING UP

Some female centipedes look after their eggs until they hatch. When little centipedes hatch, they have just seven pairs of legs, but they develop new legs as they grow bigger. Centipedes always have an odd number of leg pairs, which is why they never have exactly 100 legs.

Legs
*Centipedes have one pair of legs on each
body segment. The last pair of legs is
longer than the others. Centipedes can run
much faster than millipedes, even though
millipedes have more legs.*

GIANT CENTIPEDES

About 3,500 species of centipede exist. Giant centipedes live in rain forests around the world. They feed on frogs, spiders, birds, lizards, rodents, and even bats. Like all centipedes, they have claws that curve around their heads to inject **venom** into their prey.

The giant centipede grows to a foot (30.5 centimeters) long.

YARD AND HOUSE

During hot summer months, centipedes prefer to hide underneath plant pots, in the soil, or in any dark, cool, and damp place in the yard. However, as summer fades, they often move into the warmth of a house to avoid the cold winter.

MILLIPEDES

Millipedes are similar to centipedes, but they eat plants and usually have two pairs of legs on each body segment. There are about 10,000 species of millipede. Unlike centipedes, when millipedes feel threatened, they roll themselves into a coil.

A millipede's exoskeleton protects it like armor.

Antennae-like legs
The last set of legs look like antennae, making it difficult to tell which is the head end.

GRASSHOPPERS

A grasshopper may be difficult to see until it is startled and leaps to safety. Birds, snakes, lizards, and frogs often prey on these insects, so their fast reactions help them to survive. There are more than 10,000 species of grasshopper.

Short antennae
Two short and sensitive antennae grow from the head. They are used for touch and to smell.

Munching mouthparts
Grasshoppers are herbivores, and their mouthparts are perfect for slicing and chewing tough grass.

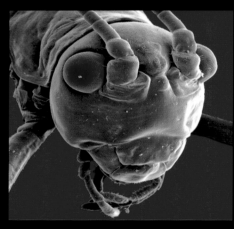

The palps can be seen just below the mouth.

SENSES

Grasshoppers have three simple eyes and two compound eyes that detect light and dark. Two sensitive palps and antennae are in front of the jaws. Grasshoppers hear sounds using a drumlike organ—the tympanal organ—found on their bodies, not their heads.

Many grasshoppers are brown or green so they are well-**camouflaged**, but others are brightly colored to warn **predators** that they taste foul.

FACT FILE

TYPE
Class: Insecta
Order: Orthoptera

DIET
Plants

FOUND
Worldwide, especially in grasslands

0   1²/₁₀ inches (30 mm)

SIZE • ⁴/₁₀ INCH– 3¹/₁₀ INCHES (1–8 CM)

MAKING MUSIC

Male grasshoppers sing to attract females at mating time. They sing by rubbing their hind legs over a ridge on their wings, and females are attracted by the sound of their chirps. Females lay eggs in the soil or in plants. When the nymphs hatch, they have soft pale bodies that quickly harden and darken in color. Nymphs look like adult grasshoppers, but they do not have wings.

JUMPERS

The long hind (back) legs of a grasshopper have large, strong muscles and a "spring" mechanism. The spring enables the legs to work like a catapult, thrusting the grasshopper forward and upward. A large grasshopper can leap one yard (1 meter) forward and 10 inches (25 centimeters) upward.

Wings
The two pairs of wings are usually folded against the body. Some wings have bold colors and are flashed at predators to scare them away.

Knee
The knee works like a spring to suddenly release power.

BUSH CRICKETS

Bush crickets belong to the same order as grasshoppers, but they have longer antennae. When they call, their chirps sound like "katy-did, katy-did," which is why they are known as katydids.

Some katydid species have red eyes.

EARWIGS

Earwigs are common yard bugs. They often hide beneath plant pots, where they stay during the day. They come out at night to hunt or search for food. About 2,000 species of earwig are found throughout the world, especially in woodlands.

HUNTERS

Earwigs are scavengers, which means they eat old or rotting plant and animal matter. They sometimes hunt and eat other small animals, using their pincerlike cerci to grab hold of their prey. Gardeners often consider earwigs to be a pest because they also feed on flowers and vegetables.

*A **mother** tends her young, keeping them safe.*

GOOD MOTHERS

Few insects look after their eggs, but earwig mothers do. They sometimes care for their young, too. Young earwigs are called nymphs. They look similar to the adults.

The hind wings are big and fan-shaped, but earwigs usually walk and do not fly.

DEFENSE

Earwigs cannot bite hard. Instead, some types of earwig defend themselves by spraying a smelly liquid from the abdomen at attackers. This liquid covers a distance of 4 inches (10 centimeters).

Earwigs have simple mouthparts.

Cerci
There is a pair of pincerlike cerci at the end of the insect's abdomen. They are straight in females and curved in males.

Body shape
An earwig's slender, flattened body is the right shape for squeezing between rocks, beneath plant pots, or into the soil. Earwigs spend winter in these places.

Wings
Tough, leathery forewings cover and protect the delicate hind wings beneath.

MOLTING

Common earwigs lay their eggs in spring. The young that hatch must grow and molt their skin several times before they become adult earwigs. When an insect molts, it sheds old skin to reveal a new layer of skin beneath. In between molts, the young earwigs are called **instars**. They must leave their mothers after they become a second instar, or they might eat them!

FACT FILE

TYPE
Class: Insecta
Order: Dermaptera

DIET
Plants and small animals

FOUND
Worldwide, especially woodlands

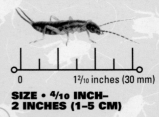

0   1²/10 inches (30 mm)

SIZE • ⁴/10 INCH–
2 INCHES (1–5 CM)

STICK INSECTS

Although stick insects are common in **tropical** forests, they also live in yards in warm parts of the world. However, they can be very difficult to find. These bugs have one of the most impressive forms of camouflage in the animal world.

CAMOUFLAGE

There are about 2,500 species of stick insect. They are also called walking sticks because they are long and sticklike, and they are perfectly shaped to hide among the twiggy parts of trees and bushes. Although they can stay perfectly still for hours, some types of stick insect sway from side to side instead so they look like twigs that are moving in a gentle breeze.

LEAF INSECTS

Like stick insects, leaf insects also belong to the order Phasmatodea. Of about 30 species of leaf insects, most are found in the forests of Southeast Asia and Australia. They are perfectly camouflaged for a life in trees or bushes, and they can sway in the breeze to complete the deception. Leaf insects have two sets of wings but use just one set to fly. When a leaf insect is resting, its wings are hidden from view.

Leaf insects are 1 to 4 inches (3 to 11 centimeters) long.

Females scatter their eggs on the ground.

EGGS

Female stick insects are usually larger than males. A female stick insect lays large eggs after mating. The eggs look like little pieces of wood. They are camouflaged to protect them from predators.

Mimicry
The way that a stick insect pretends to be a stick is called mimicry.

Long Body
Some species are more than 20 inches (50 centimeters) long, making them the longest known insects. Chan's megastick is the largest species. One measured 22.3 inches (56.7 centimeters).

The goliath stick insect can grow to 10 inches (25 centimeters) long, and it has large wings. This giant bug lives in Australian forests and yards. It favors eucalyptus trees, which are indigenous (native) to Australia.

Legs
Stick insects' legs are long, ridged, and sometimes spiky. The forelegs can be held in front of the head.

PRAYING MANTISES

Mantises are some of the world's most incredible predators. They may be small, but these bugs are fearless hunters with lightning-quick reactions and lethal weapons: powerful jaws and slashing, grabbing claws. They are impressive killers. The females even turn on males, and eat them.

Flower mantises can mimic petals, buds, and leaves.

SPINY FLOWER MANTIS

Flower mantises mimic flowers. This helps them to be perfectly camouflaged as they lie in wait for bugs to come near.

SILENT BUT DEADLY

Like many other bug predators, mantises lie in wait for their prey. They remain motionless on a plant until another insect comes close. Then they whip their spiked forelimbs forward and grab the prey. Mantises eat their prey alive.

Small head
The head is small, but the compound eyes are large and face forward. They are perfect for seeing prey clearly.

Long antennae
The two sensitive antennae are long and thin.

Turning head
Mantises can turn their heads around to see what is happening behind them, and escape if a predator is nearby.

Green or brown
The tough outer shell, called the exoskeleton, is usually green or brown, but mantises can even be pink. Their color camouflages them when they are on plants.

⊕ PRAYING POSE
Mantises are described as "praying" because they hold up their forelimbs, as if they are in prayer. The mantis's legs and wings are long and slender. Some species do not have wings. Among the more than 2,000 kinds of mantises are the the Texas unicorn mantis and Carolina mantis.

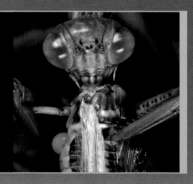

An insect's chewing mouthparts are called **mandibles**. A mantis's mouthparts are tough enough to chew beetles and scorpions.

FACT FILE

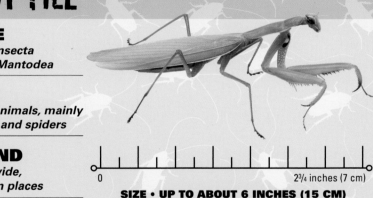

TYPE
Class: Insecta
Order: Mantodea

DIET
Small animals, mainly insects and spiders

FOUND
Worldwide, in warm places

0   2³/₄ inches (7 cm)

SIZE • UP TO ABOUT 6 INCHES (15 CM)

COCKROACHES

Cockroaches are some of the world's most prolific animals. They live in yards, houses, and woodlands, but they can also survive long periods of time in extreme conditions, with no food or water. There are about 4,500 different kinds of cockroach, and some of those are household pests.

SCAVENGERS

Cockroaches do not hunt for prey. They are not fussy eaters and will devour almost anything they find, including rotting food, dead animals, and plants. Cockroaches easily pick up **bacteria** on their feet when they feed, and they can spread diseases such as salmonella. Salmonella causes an infection in the intestines, resulting in diarrhea in humans.

WARNING

Most cockroaches are dull brown, but some have bright yellow, red, or orange markings. The vibrant colors warn predators that these species can release a foul-smelling liquid from their bodies.

Yellow and red are nature's warning colors.

Flat body
The body is flattened for squeezing into small, dark spaces. It has an oval shape.

Wings
Delicate hind wings, sometimes used for flying, are protected by

⊕ BABY BUGS

Female cockroaches produce up to 50 sticky egg cases in their lifetime, with each case containing 12 to 14 eggs. Some species carry the case on their abdomen until the eggs are ready to hatch. Others do not lay their eggs at all but keep them inside their bodies and give birth to live young. The young are small and white, but they quickly grow. Cockroaches live up to two years.

Cockroaches have compound eyes and can see well in the dark. Their antennae are long and made up of many segments.

Pronotum
*A shield-shaped body part covers the thorax and protects the head. It is called a **pronotum**.*

FACT FILE

TYPE
Class: Insecta
Order: Blattodea

DIET
Plants, and anything else they find

FOUND
Worldwide, especially warm, dark places

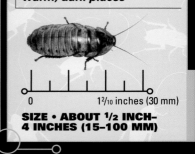

0   1²/₁₀ inches (30 mm)

**SIZE • ABOUT ¹/₂ INCH–
4 INCHES (15–100 MM)**

BIG PESTS

American cockroaches are considered one of the biggest pest cockroaches and can grow to 1½ inches (4 centimeters) in length.

These pests are common in city dumps and restaurants.

actually ants. In fact, they are more closely related to cockroaches. Termites are described as "social insects" because they live in large groups, called **colonies**, and they share the work of looking after the young. Only around 300 of about 3,000 species of termites are pests.

⊕ WOOD EATERS

These small insects make their homes in soil or in wood. They eat plant material, which they are able to digest thanks to special bacteria in their guts. Termites help to break down dead and rotting woody plants. They can be a problem to people because they often damage wood sheds, fences, and houses.

Exoskeleton
Soldier termites have thicker, stronger exoskeletons than worker termites, which often have pale, soft bodies.

Termite mounds stay cool and dry inside.

TERMITE MOUNDS

In tropical areas, termites can build huge mounds from soil, where they live. The tallest can reach 20 feet (6 meters).

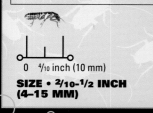
COLONIES

Hundreds, thousands, or even millions of termites
can live in one colony. A colony contains eggs,
young termites (called nymphs), workers, soldiers,
a king, and a queen. The queen lays 20,000 or
more eggs every day. Workers provide food for the
other members of the colony, while soldiers use
their large mouthparts to defend the colony.
Soldier termites have such large jaws that they
cannot feed themselves.

Thorax
*Three pairs of
legs are attached
to the thorax.
Some termites
have wings, and
these also grow
from the thorax.*

***The strong
mouthparts** are
adapted for
chewing. The
antennae
are small.*

Abdomen
*The large abdomen contains the gut,
where plant material is digested.*

***Worker termites** are sterile
and cannot reproduce.*

WORKER TERMITES
Workers collect food, which
they share with other colony
members. Workers cause
most of the damage to
homes and other buildings.

GIANT WATER BUGS

The eggs carried by their father are called a brood. He looks after his eggs because if they are not protected, they are more likely to be eaten by other animals.

Giant water bugs are related to aphids, termites, and cicadas, but they live in freshwater. They are common in slow-moving streams, lakes, and ponds. They are also known as electric light bugs and toe-biters because they are attracted to electric lights, and sometimes they bite people. There are about 150 species of giant water bug.

⊕ HARD-WORKING FATHERS

Giant water bugs do something very unusual for an insect: The males take care of the eggs. The female giant water bug lays her eggs on the back of their father. He carries the eggs around until they are ready to hatch.

Body shape
The body is large and oval-shaped. Beneath the wings is a space where the bug keeps a trapped air bubble to help it breathe underwater.

Water bugs can dive below the water surface.

SWIMMING LEGS

Water bugs have sharp claws on their front legs and hairs on their two pairs of swimming legs. The hairs increase the surface area of the legs, making it easier for the bug to row through the water.

HUNGRY BUGS

Giant water bugs have big appetites, and they have the power and weapons to attack and kill large prey. They mostly eat insects and other invertebrates, tadpoles, and small fish, but some species attack baby turtles and small snakes.

Powerful legs
The front pair of legs has claws for catching prey.

Mouthparts
Their mouthparts work like a sharp bea to pierce through the skin of the bug's prey

Muddy color
The dull color and body shape help the bug to mimic a dead leaf on the surface of the water. This makes it easier for a bug to ambush its prey and hide from

FACT FILE

TYPE
Class: Insecta
Order: Hemiptera

DIET
Small animals

FOUND
Worldwide in freshwater

0   About 1¹/₂ inches (40 mm)

**SIZE • ABOUT ¹/₂ INCH–
4 INCHES (15–100 MM)**

FROGHOPPERS

Froghoppers live on plants and are especially common in yards, gardens, parks, and meadows, where they feed on plants and plants' **sap**. They are superb jumpers and can leap out of danger when predators, such as birds, come too close.

BRIGHT COLORS

Most froghoppers are green or brown, but some types such as this red-and-black froghopper are brightly colored. This species grows up to $^4/_{10}$ inch (11 millimeters) long and is common in Europe.

This froghopper lives in grassy places such as backyards.

Pronotum
The shield-shaped pronotum is larger than the head and helps to protect it.

*Beneath this frothy layer of cuckoo spit, a froghopper nymph is hiding. The spit contains sap, which the nymph has sucked out of the plant. It is made up of water and **nutrients**—and this honeybee has discovered that it makes an easy energy drink!*

BUGS

Froghoppers belong to a group of insects called bugs (although the word "bug" is also used to describe all sorts of creepy-crawlies). There are nearly 90,000 species of bugs. They have two pairs of wings and mouthparts that are shaped for piercing and sucking. Many garden bugs are pests because they damage plants.

Folded wings
Most froghoppers hold their wings against their body, protecting the soft abdomen.

FACT FILE

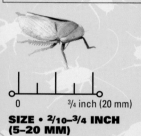

○ **TYPE**
Class: Insecta
Order: Hemiptera

○ **DIET**
Plant sap

○ **FOUND**
Worldwide, especially in warmer places

0   ³/₄ inch (20 mm)

SIZE • ²/₁₀–³/₄ INCH (5–20 MM)

Legs
There are six pairs of legs. There are spines on the hind legs. Froghoppers can leap up to 27 inches (70 centimeters) in a single jump.

CUCKOO SPIT

Young froghoppers are called nymphs. The nymphs coat themselves in thick froth, which they make by pushing air bubbles into a liquid that comes out of the bugs' **anus**. This froth is called cuckoo spit. It covers a nymph and protects it from predators while it sucks plant sap. It also stops it from drying out in the sunshine.

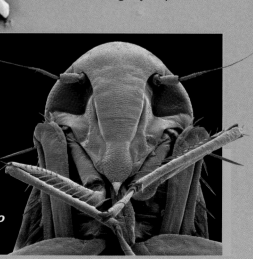

UP CLOSE
Froghoppers have large, round eyes. The mouthparts of nymphs are perfect for sucking sap, but adults eat leaves and stems too.

Froghoppers are also called *spittlebugs*.

CICADAS

Cicadas can be heard long before they can be seen, especially when they gather together in groups at mating time. Adult cicadas can fly and are common around trees and in gardens. Their nymphs, however, are harder to see because they live underground, where they feed on roots.

NOISY BUGS

Male cicadas are the loudest insects with songs. They can be heard more than 400 yards away. Their songs are so loud that when they sing together, the noise can be painful to the human ear. Males sing by vibrating a membrane on their abdomen so fast that it creates pulses of sound, which are amplified (made louder) by a space beneath. Males sing to attract females at mating time.

Body shape
The body is large, heavy, and oval-shaped. Two pairs of wings fold back against the body.

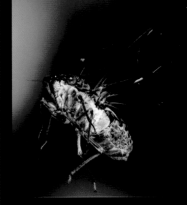

Cicadas are heavy bugs and noisy flyers.

FLYING
The forewings are longer than the hind wings. They are usually **transparent** (see-through) or have some markings for camouflage.

LONG LIFE

Cicadas are also the longest-living bugs. Periodical cicadas may live underground as nymphs for 13 to 17 years before they turn into adults. The adults mate, lay eggs, and die within a few weeks of the eggs hatching.

Mouthparts
Like other bugs, cicadas have long sucking mouthparts. They feed by piercing plants and sucking.

FACT FILE

TYPE
Class: Insecta
Order: Hemiptera

DIET
Plants

FOUND
Woodlands worldwide, especially in warmer places

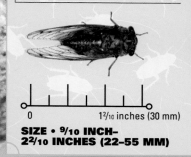

0   1²/₁₀ inches (30 mm)

**SIZE • ⁹/₁₀ INCH–
2²/₁₀ INCHES (22–55 MM)**

The dark marks behind the head are false eyespots. The cicada is soft-shelled and cannot protect itself, so it relies upon its eyespots to frighten away predators.

MOLTING

When a nymph is ready for adulthood, it must shed its old skin. This takes a few hours. When the new adult emerges, it is soft and pale. It dries out its new exoskeleton, which darkens as it dries.

When a cicada molts, it cannot fly and is at high risk from predators.

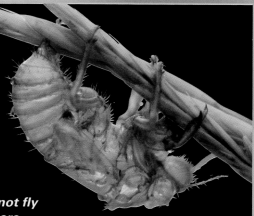

POND SKATERS

A garden pond may seem peaceful and motionless—until you get close and look carefully at its surface. Groups of pond skaters scoot across the water using their legs to sense any movement, which signals that food—in the form of other insects—is nearby.

WATER STRIDERS

Pond skaters are also known as water striders. They use their long, thin legs to spread their weight over water so they can skate along its surface without sinking. Operating like a pair of oars, the middle pair of legs do most of the work.

Wings
Like all members of the bug family, pond skaters have two pairs of wings. They can fly to a new pond if their own pond becomes too crowded with other pond skaters.

Legs
The forelegs are short and used for catching prey or grabbing hold of dead insects. The hind legs are used like rudders to steer the insect as it skates.

PREDATORS

Pond skaters are predators that feed on other insects. They grab them with claws and stab them with piercing mouthparts. They also feed on dead insects and spiders that they find.

As it scoots across the pond, a pond skater searches for food.

SURVIVAL

Pond skaters must leap to escape hungry predators such as birds. They can survive cold winters, when ponds freeze over, by hibernating. They emerge from hibernation in spring to mate and lay their eggs.

Dark bodies
There are at least 750 species of pond skater. Their dark bodies are covered in hairs.

FACT FILE

TYPE
Class: Insecta
Order: Hemiptera

DIET
Insects and spiders

FOUND
Worldwide in freshwater

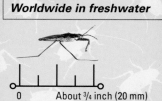

0   About ¾ inch (20 mm)

SIZE • 8/100 INCH–1⁴/10 INCHES (2–35 MM)

The front legs on a pond skater's body help it to sense any vibrations on the water surface. The legs have hairs that repel water so the insect can stay dry.

NYMPHS

Pond skater nymphs hatch from eggs and molt several times before they are adults. Between the molts, they go through five stages, known as instars. Adults sometimes eat the nymphs.

Instars can also skate across the water's surface.

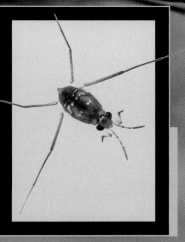

SHIELD BUGS

Shield bugs are sometimes called stink bugs because they are able to make foul smells. There are at least 5,500 species of shield bug. Most species use their sucking mouthparts to feed on plants, often damaging them—especially if many shield bugs gather on one plant. However, some shield bugs are predators and attack caterpillars.

TOXIC SHOCK

Any bird that tries to eat a shield bug gets a nasty shock when the bug releases foul-smelling liquids from between its first and second pairs of legs. The smell is similar to that of moldy almonds, so humans do not usually find it disgusting. In some countries, stink bugs are cooked and eaten.

Red shield bugs do not need to hide from predators.

FOUL TASTE

These bugs have clever ways to stay alive. Some are colored to warn predators to stay away. Bold colors, especially red and yellow, suggest that an insect tastes bad or has a stinger, so these bugs are often left alone. Shield bugs survive the cold winter weather by hibernating.

FACT FILE

TYPE
Class: Insecta
Order: Hemiptera

DIET
Mostly plants, although some hunt as adults

FOUND
Worldwide

0   6/10 inch (15 mm)

SIZE • 2/10–1 INCH (5–25 MM)

HUNGRY NYMPHS

When the nymphs hatch from their eggs, they eat their egg cases, which their mother has coated with bacteria. The nymphs need the bacteria in their guts to digest the plant sap they will eat. Nymphs look like adults, and they can also make a stink to defend themselves.

The newly laid eggs stick to the surface of a leaf.

Pronotum
The pronotum—the first segment of the thorax—is large and may have square edges.

Wings
The forewings are thicker and stronger than the hind wings. They protect the softer hind wings, which are hidden beneath.

TAKING CARE

Females can lay up to 400 eggs in their lifetime. Unlike most insects, shield bug mothers guard their eggs from predators. Some species sit on their eggs, like a bird hatching its brood. When they hatch, the nymphs feed on the plant they are on, but some become predators.

Body shap
The body is shaped like a shiel giving the shield bug its commo name. Most shield bugs a green, so they are hard see on a plant, unles they are basking the su

Firebugs are shield bugs with distinctive red and black markings, which also give them their other common name of clown-faced bug.

WOODLICE

These familiar bugs are not insects: they are crustaceans. Woodlice are closely related to animals that live in water, such as crabs, lobsters, and shrimp. Woodlice are also known as sow bugs.

HABITAT

Although woodlice originally lived in Europe, they are now also found in North America and elsewhere around the world. They need damp, cool habitats, so they hide between rocks, in the soil, in piles of leaves and compost, or under plant pots. Woodlice also squeeze into gaps beneath tree bark.

MOLTING

Like other arthropods, woodlice must shed their old skin as they grow. This is called molting, and they do it in two halves: They shed the back half first.

The old skin appears pale as it lifts off the body.

Legs

Segments

The body is oval-shaped and divided into segments that have "armor-plating" for protection. Woodlice are dull colored, usually gray or glossy black.

PILL BUGS

Pill bugs are woodlice that roll themselves up into a ball when they are disturbed. This may save them from being attacked and eaten by predators.

Pill bugs are also known as pill woodlice.

FACT FILE

TYPE
Class: Malacostraca
Order: Isopoda

DIET
Plants

FOUND
Worldwide in dark, damp places

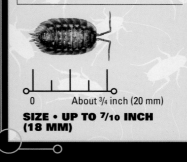

0   About ³/₄ inch (20 mm)

SIZE • UP TO ⁷/₁₀ INCH (18 MM)

Antennae
The antennae look crooked and tap the ground as the woodlouse walks

A mother keeps her eggs in a pouch beneath her body until they are ready to hatch. The babies are small and white, but they look similar to adults

FOOD HABITS

Woodlice feed on dead plant matter, so they often make their homes in compost heaps, where they help break down rotting leaves. They do not have good eyesight, so they find their food by using their senses of touch and smell

SCARAB BEETLES

With at least 30,000 species, one of the largest groups of beetles is the scarab beetle group. These insects live all over the world in many kinds of habitats, from parks and yards to deserts and rain forests. The group includes some of the largest insects. The Hercules beetle can grow to 7 inches (18 centimeters), including its "horns."

Head shape
Some species have a simple head shape with mandibles for eating plants. Others have large heads with horns for fighting, or they have shovel-shaped heads for moving plant material and dung.

Antennae
The sensitive antennae are often clubbed at the tips, or broad and fan-shaped.

BIG AND STRONG

Most scarab beetles in yards and parks go about their business unnoticed. However, some are insect record-breakers. The heaviest of all insects, for example, are rhino beetles, which have giant larvae that weigh more than 7 ounces (200 grams). One species of **dung** beetle can lift more than 1,100 times its own weight!

RHINO BEETLE
Rhino beetles are huge and strong. They are capable of lifting something 850 times heavier than themselves!

Males use their strange "horns" to fight one another and to dig.

IN THE GARDEN

The larvae of many scarab beetles, such as chafers, feed on backyard plants—especially grass roots. They are pests because they can do great damage. Others are welcome in the yard or garden because they feed on old and rotting plant material, helping to return the nutrients to the soil, so more plants will grow.

A male fans out his antennae to pick up more scent.

HAIRY ANTENNAE

This European cockchafer is also known as a May bug or a June bug. "Chafer" is an old word for "chew." The males have huge antennae, which they can use to smell females. They can smell females that are far away.

FACT FILE

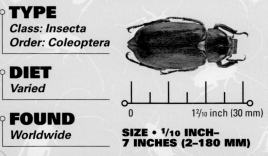

TYPE
Class: Insecta
Order: Coleoptera

DIET
Varied

FOUND
Worldwide

0   1²/₁₀ inch (30 mm)

SIZE • ¹/₁₀ INCH–
7 INCHES (2–180 MM)

DUNG BEETLES

Dung beetles collect feces (dung) and lay their eggs inside, so their larvae can safely feed on it. They use the sun and stars to help them find their way as they move the dung to a safe place.

Dung beetles roll dung into balls so it is easy to move.

TIGER BEETLES

Tiger beetles belong to a huge group of beetles called ground beetles. There are about 30,000 species of ground beetle. Tiger beetles are found all over the world, in all types of habitats. Some tiger beetles live in trees, but most prefer to stay on the ground, especially in sandy, dry places.

⊕ RECORD BREAKER

Tiger beetles, which include about 2,000 species, are the fastest-running insects in the world. The Australian tiger beetle holds the record for the fastest species, with a top speed of 5.6 miles per hour (9 kilometers per hour).

Green tiger beetles live throughout Europe.

TYPES OF TIGER BEETLE

Tiger beetles are mostly very similar in size and shape. Some are plain brown or black, others—such as this green tiger beetle—have a metallic shininess, called iridescence.

Color
This is a blue-spotted tiger beetle, with shiny blue-green elytra (wing cases). Many tiger beetles are brightly colored, but some are dull.

Tiger beetles run so fast that they become blind while they are in pursuit. They must stop midrun so they can get a good look before they set off again.

FACT FILE

TYPE
Class: Insecta
Order: Coleoptera

DIET
Invertebrates, especially insects and spiders

FOUND
Worldwide

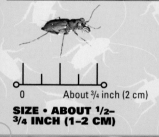

0   About ¾ inch (2 cm)

SIZE • ABOUT ½– ¾ INCH (1–2 CM)

Big eyes
Most tiger beetles are **nocturnal**, so they need large eyes for spotting prey in the dark.

Body shape
The body is long and slender and raised off the ground by three pairs of long legs. The three body parts (head, thorax, and abdomen) are clearly separated.

With its large eyes, the beetle can see in all directions.

FIERCE HUNTERS

Once a tiger beetle has caught up with its prey, it grabs hold of it and begins to crush it with massive, toothed jaws. It then pours its spit over its victim. The spit begins to dissolve the flesh, digesting it even before it is inside the beetle's guts.

UP CLOSE

Seen up close, these beetles have a fearsome appearance. Their mandibles (grasping jaws) are large and curved. They can crunch prey easily.

STAG BEETLES

Stag beetles are easy to recognize. They have large, shiny bodies and huge mandibles that are used for fighting, rather than eating. As adults, they lumber along the ground, searching for mates. Stag beetles can fly, but they are cumbersome and noisy as they propel themselves slowly through the air.

FIGHTING

Males use their horns to grab one another and wrestle, fighting over mating space, or territory. Their huge heads are packed with muscles so they can push and shove their rivals. They usually emerge from pupation before the females, so when the females arrive, the winning males already have their mating space ready.

Body shape
The body is clearly separated into a head, thorax, and abdomen. Most stag beetles are black, brown, or red-brown. Some tropical species have iridescent exoskeletons.

ENDANGERED
There are about 1,300 species of stag beetle and some of those, such as this European stag beetle, are **endangered**. Their habitats have been destroyed, and they are easy prey for large animals such as cats and dogs to kill.

Adult European stag beetles die before the winter sets in.

Giant jaws
The jaws of a stag beetle resemble the huge antlers of a male deer (or "stag"), giving this group of insects their common name.

⊕ LIFE CYCLE

Eggs are laid in old trees or rotting wood. The large, white **grubs** can spend three years or more feeding on wood, before pupating inside a **cocoon** the size of an orange. They emerge as adults from spring to early summer. The adults do not usually feed, although they sometimes drink **nectar** from flowers or tree sap. Adult stag beetles die soon after the eggs are laid.

Antennae
The antennae come out from either side of the head, where they are less likely to get damaged during a fight.

Males have larger mandibles than females. However, the females are known to bite toes, giving a painful nip if they are disturbed.

The giant larvae of stag beetles need to feed and grow undisturbed for a long time. Gardeners often leave piles of old wood in a corner of the garden so beetles can make a home for their larvae there.

CAT FLEAS

It is almost impossible to see cat fleas lurking in the backyard because they are tiny and hide out of sight. These minibeasts prefer to live indoors on a warm animal's body. However, sometimes fleas have to survive outdoors, waiting in dry, shady places for a pet cat or dog to pass by.

Fleas are able to scamper through fur because they are paper-thin. A slender body can pass between hairs easily and is difficult to squash.

THE HOST

Once a flea has sensed a warm-blooded animal nearby, it jumps aboard and nestles among the cat or dog's fur. Its unsuspecting host brings the flea into the home, and the flea soon starts to suck the pet's blood. This is when a female flea lays her eggs.

Legs
A flea's legs contain a rubbery material called resilin. This allows fleas to leap about 150 times their own length.

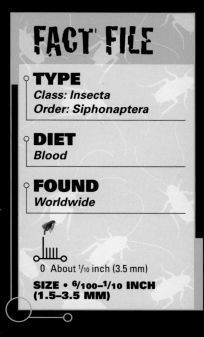
Mouthparts
*A flea uses its mouthparts to pierce a hole
in the host's skin and suck the blood.*

⊕ LIFE CYCLE

Flea eggs slip off the host's
body and land in a pet's bed,
or on a carpet, where they grow
into larvae. The larvae build silk
cocoons around themselves, and
go through **metamorphosis**.
Once they become adults, the
fleas must jump aboard a host
animal, but they can survive
for many weeks without food
while they wait to find one.

LARVAE

Flea larvae have no eyes or legs; this is just a feeding
stage in the life cycle of the flea. The larvae eat almost
anything they find, including dried skin and adult flea poo.

**A flea larvae
feeds for
about two to
three weeks.**

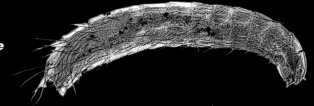

ROBBER FLIES

Robber flies love warm, sunny yards where plenty of other little animals live. These insects are famous for their large appetites and hunting skills. There are more than 7,000 species of robber fly.

PEST KILLERS

Robber flies fly quickly toward their prey, grabbing it and injecting it with toxic saliva (spit), using their **proboscis** to pierce the victim's body. The saliva stops the victim from moving and begins to dissolve its body, so the flies can suck up this liquid meal. Robber flies can suck out the insides of a bug in less than 30 minutes.

Wings
All insects in the order Diptera *have just one pair of wings. Behind them, the hind wings have become a pair of balancing organs called halteres. Robber flies have broad wings.*

Body shape
Some robber flies have large, stocky bodies, but others are slender and delicate. They are gray, black, or brown.

PREDATORS

Robber flies hunt insects, such as scarab beetles, and they also attack useful insects, such as bees and wasps. They usually hunt flying insects, and they can kill animals bigger than themselves.

This robber fly caught a dragonfly and is now feeding.

Proboscis
The mouthpart is called a proboscis. It is strong and spikelike.

FACT FILE

TYPE
Class: Insecta
Order: Diptera

DIET
Insects

FOUND
Worldwide, especially warm places

0   About 1 inch (25 mm)

SIZE • 1/10 INCH–
2 INCHES (3–50 MM)

HUGE EYES

Like many predators, these insects need good eyesight to find and follow their prey. Robber flies have compound eyes made of many lenses.

It has huge eyes, but this fly cannot see the color red.

Bristled legs
The legs are strong and covered in bristles. Robber flies use their legs to grab hold of prey.

BLOWFLIES

There are about 150,000 species of fly in the world and just 1,500 of those are blowflies. Blowflies are a group of disease-spreading insects that are common in homes, parks, and yards. They are known as bluebottles and greenbottles because of the color of their abdomens and thoraxes.

LIFE CYCLE

Adult females lay their eggs in rotting plants, food, and animal bodies. The eggs hatch quickly and the small, white maggots feed on the food around them. When the flies are ready to turn into adults, they burrow into soil and **pupate**, building a protective brown shell around themselves as they metamorphose.

CLAWS

Like other flies, a blowfly is nimble on its feet and can walk on vertical surfaces, and can even walk upside-down.

Blowflies have claws on their feet for gripping.

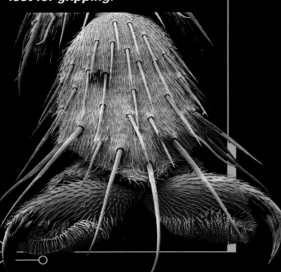

Thorax
The thorax is dark and has short spikes that are used to defend the fly from predators, such as birds and bats.

Antennae
The antennae are short and sensitive to strong smells such as nectar or rotting animals.

Wings
Of the 150,000 fly species in the world, just 1,500 are blowflies. These insects are good flyers.

⊕ EATING HABITS

Some blowfly maggots prey on ants and other small invertebrates, although some adults burrow into the flesh of living animals to lay their eggs there, especially if they find a wound on the animal's skin. When the eggs hatch just 12 hours later, the maggots start to feed on the flesh of the animal.

Adults suck up liquid using their spongelike mouthparts, and they often feed on rotting food or fallen fruit.

Bristles
The plump body and the legs are covered with short bristles.

MOSQUITOES

Mosquitoes may be small, but they are one of the deadliest animals on the planet, spreading diseases such as malaria and dengue fever. These diseases infect humans, and malaria-spreading mosquitoes are found all over the world. Adult mosquitoes feed on blood and nectar.

FACT FILE

TYPE
Class: Insecta
Order: Diptera

DIET
Blood and nectar

FOUND
Worldwide, especially warm places

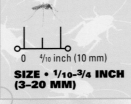

0   4/10 inch (10 mm)

SIZE • 1/10-3/4 INCH (3–20 MM)

Abdomen
The flies are dull colored but the abdomen of a female appears pink-red after it has eaten a blood meal.

HOUSE MOSQUITOES

The northern house mosquito is common in backyards and homes of North America. These insects suck blood from birds, humans, and other warm-blooded animals. They often spend winter in houses.

Mosquitoes inject painkillers so victims do not feel the bite.

LIFE CYCLE

Only adult female mosquitoes drink blood. They need this food to lay their eggs. Eggs are placed in still or stagnant water such as garden ponds, drains, buckets, and watering cans. The larvae live in water and turn into pupae before emerging as flying adults.

Wings
The single pair of wings is attached near the rear-end of the thorax.

MALARIA
Some mosquitoes have a micro-organism called plasmodium in their saliva. When these mosquitoes bite, the plasmodium is passed on and causes malaria.

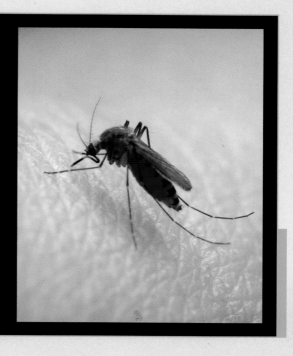

Malaria causes about 600,000 human deaths a year.

Antennae
The super-sensitive antennae help a mosquito to find its food. These insects can detect a human's breath, in the dark, from 30 yards away.

Legs
Each of a mosquito's six legs can hold 23 times its body weight.

Larvae feed on tiny pond plants and bacteria.

WRIGGLERS
Mosquito larvae are called wrigglers because of the way they swim. They hang from the surface of the water with a breathing tube poking into the air.

Proboscis
Mosquitoes use their needlelike mouthparts to pierce flesh and suck up blood. Their spit makes the wound swollen and itchy.

CRANE FLIES

With long, gangly legs, crane flies—commonly called mosquito hawks—resemble large mosquitoes. They belong to an old and prolific group of insects of about 15,000 species worldwide. Crane flies like damp habitats, and they are often found on damp lawns in the early morning.

LEATHERJACKETS
Young crane flies are called leatherjackets. They are pests in a garden or yard because they live in the soil, eating plant roots—especially grass roots. Leatherjackets can also live in water.

This leatherjacket will become a pupa and then an adult.

FAVORITE FOOD
Crane flies are not fast flyers, and they have no powerful way to protect themselves, such as a toxic bite or sting. They are a favorite food of other garden animals, especially birds, which poke around in soil looking for leatherjackets to eat.

BALANCING ACT
Most flying insects with long legs use their limbs to spread their weight on water or to feed, but crane flies probably use them to balance as they fly. They may also use their legs as feelers to help them find their way in the dark and avoid bumping into things.

Wings
There is one pair of long, transparent wings with distinct "veins." In the larger species, the **wingspan** can be up to 4 inches (10 centimeters).

UP CLOSE
Seen up close, a crane fly's head looks extraordinary, with its huge eyes and long, beaklike mouthparts. Adults, however, rarely eat and live for just a few weeks.

Crane flies have large compound eyes.

FACT FILE

TYPE
Class: Insecta
Order: Diptera

DIET
Plants and nectar

FOUND
Worldwide, especially damp habitats

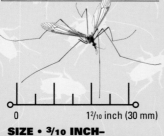

0   1²/₁₀ inch (30 mm)

**SIZE • ³/₁₀ INCH–
3 INCHES (7–77 MM)**

Sometimes crane flies drink a flower's nectar. When they fly between flowers, they carry **pollen**. This is called pollination and helps flowers to grow seeds.

LIGHTNING BUGS

Once the Sun has gone down, lightning bugs produce incredible flashes of light in trees. They are also known as fireflies or glowworms, but these insects are not worms, flies, or bugs; they are beetles.

Larvae live for about one year.

LARVAE

Adults eat very little, but the larvae feed on invertebrates. The larvae also glow, and in some places they are called glowworms. They look similar to adults.

Wings
Males have wings, but some females are wingless.

MAKING LIGHT

These small nocturnal beetles have special places on their abdomens that make a cold, green light. At twilight, orange lights glow better, so some fireflies make orange light instead. The lights attract mates, and each species flashes its lights in a pattern that helps mates of its own species to find it.

Body shape
The body is a typical beetle shape, with an oval and exoskeleton. Most beetles have hard exoskeletons, but lightning bugs have soft bodies.

Head
The head is hidden beneath a large pronotum. The antennae are threadlike.

LIGHT ORGANS
The special places where light is made are called the light organs. They are on the underside of the fifth, sixth, and seventh segments of the abdomen.

The green glow can be switched off and on.

Legs
These beetles have three pairs of legs with each leg ending in a single claw. (Double claws are more common in other beetles.)

TRICKERY
Some female lightning bugs flash lights in a way that is typical of other species, so curious males come close to investigate with the hope of mating. In fact, the females lure them close just to eat them!

FUSSY FEMALES
Although both males and females can flash, males flash more or brighter. Females prefer to mate with males who make the most flashes or the brightest lights.

Females must choose which male to mate with.

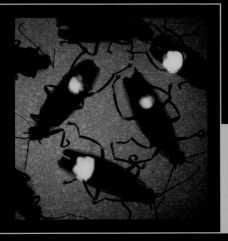

HAWK MOTHS

Hawk moths are found in most regions of the world, but they are most common in warm places. More than 1,000 species of hawk moth exist, and most of them are fast flyers. Hawk moths visit yards and parks to feed on flower nectar and lay their eggs.

Antennae
The sensitive antennae of hawk moths are not as furry as those of other moths. Males have hairier antennae than females, and they use them to find females by their smell.

FACT FILE

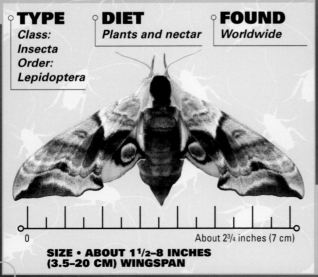

TYPE
Class: Insecta
Order: Lepidoptera

DIET
Plants and nectar

FOUND
Worldwide

0   About 2³/4 inches (7 cm)

SIZE • ABOUT 1¹/2–8 INCHES (3.5–20 CM) WINGSPAN

⊕ LARVAE

Hawk moths are large moths, and their larvae can grow to 4 inches (10 centimeters) long. The larvae feed on plants. Some of them are pests because they damage crops such as tomato plants. They are called hornworms because they have a spike, or horn, at the end of the abdomen.

⊕ POLLINATORS

Like many insects, hawk moths have an important job to do in the garden. They are pollinators: When they flit between flowers, they carry pollen with them. This fertilizes the flowers so fruits and seeds can grow.

Wings
The wings are long and elegant. Hawk moths can reach speeds of more than 30 miles per hour (48 kilometers per hour) and migrate long distances.

HOVERING

Hawk moths are superb flyers that can hover—staying in one place—while they feed from a flower. They can also suddenly swoop to the side to avoid predators such as birds.

FLOWER FEEDERS

Most garden moths are active at night. Hawk moths can sometimes be seen in the day, often feeding on flowers, although they are more active in the mornings and evenings.

Insects are most active on warm, sunny days.

Eyespots
Butterflies and moths sometimes have bold patterns, called eyespots, on their wings. The insects flash their wings to reveal the eyespots and startle predators.

TICKS

Cats and dogs that stay outside often fall prey to blood-sucking ticks. These invertebrates belong to the same group as spiders, but they live very different lifestyles. About 700 species of ticks can be found almost everywhere mammals and birds live.

⊕ PARASITE

Ticks live on another animal, and they do it harm. Animals like this are called parasites, and the animals they harm are called their hosts. Garden ticks often attach themselves to pets, but they can also feed on humans.

FEEDING

The hypostome is barbed so that it sticks hard into the flesh and is very difficult to remove.

The mouth is in the center, and the palps are on either side.

Shield
A tick has a tough exoskeleton made up of plates. The one on its back is called a shield, or dorsal plate. The exoskeleton on its underside is softer so it can stretch during a blood meal.

Body shape
Ticks have two body parts: the head with mouthparts and the idiosoma, with the legs and digestive and reproductive systems.

Ticks can be dangerous. As they feed, they can pass on nasty diseases to their host.

⊕ LIFE CYCLE

Ticks sit on plants with their legs out, waiting for a host to walk by so they can grab hold of the fur. They then begin to feed by piercing the flesh and sucking blood. Eggs are laid on the ground, and young ticks must find hosts to feed on.

Legs
Ticks have four pairs of legs, just like spiders and mites. Their larvae have six legs. Tick legs have special organs that can detect the breath, heat, or smell of a nearby host.

Mouthparts
A tick's piercing and sucking mouthpart is called a hypostome.

FACT FILE

TYPE
Class: Arachnida
Order: Parasitiformes

DIET
Blood

FOUND
Worldwide

0   ⁴/₁₀ inch (10 mm)

SIZE • ⁸/₁₀₀–⁴/₁₀ INCH (2–10 MM)

GLOSSARY

ABDOMEN
The hind part of an invertebrate's body that comes after the thorax.

ANTENNAE
A pair of sensitive feelers on the top or front of an invertebrate's head.

ANUS
The end of an animal's digestive system. This is where feces or solid waste pass out of the body.

ARTHROPODS
Invertebrates that have exoskeletons and pairs of jointed legs. Spiders and insects are arthropods.

BACTERIA
Tiny living things that are made of just one cell.

CAMOUFLAGE
The way an animal can be colored or patterned so it is hidden in its habitat.

COCOON
A silky case spun by some insects when they pupate.

COLONIES
Groups of animals that live together. Bees, ants, and termites live in colonies.

COMPOST
Yard or food waste, such as fallen leaves or leftover vegetables, which is collected and left to rot. Eventually, it can be dug back into the soil to help new plants to grow.

COMPOUND EYES
Eyes made up of many lenses. Most insects have compound eyes, but humans have just one lens in each eye.

DUNG
Animal feces or solid waste.

ENDANGERED
Describes a species of animal that is in danger of becoming extinct (dying out forever).

EXOSKELETON
An arthropod's tough outer shell.

GRUBS
Maggots, or larvae, especially of flies and beetles.

HABITAT
The place where an animal usually lives.

HIBERNATING
Spending the cold winter months in a state of deep rest, which is like sleep. Hibernating helps animals to survive a time when little food is available for them to eat.

INSECTS
Arthropods that have three distinct body segments—head, thorax, and abdomen. Insects also have three pairs of legs. Most insects have one or two pairs of wings.

INSTARS
Young invertebrates between molts.

INVERTEBRATES
Animals that do not have a backbone (spine). Animals that do have a spine are called vertebrates.

LARVAE
Young invertebrates. Many larvae look very different from the adults.

MANDIBLES
An arthropod's crushing or slicing mouthparts.

METAMORPHOSIS
The time when an insect changes from being a larva to an adult.

MOLTING
When an animal sheds its old skin, revealing its new skin beneath.

NECTAR
A sugary liquid made by flowers to attract insects and other invertebrates.

NOCTURNAL
Active at night.

NUTRIENTS
The goodness contained in a food. Nutrients are needed to live and grow.

NYMPHS
The young of some insects. Unlike larvae, nymphs often look like adults.

POLLEN
The yellow powder in a flower. Pollen fertilizes the eggs in a flower, so they can grow into seeds.

PREDATORS
Animals that hunt, kill, and eat other animals.

PREY
An animal that is hunted, killed, and eaten by other animals.

PROBOSCIS
The strawlike, sucking mouthpart used by some insects to feed.

PRONOTUM
A platelike structure on some insects. It covers the thorax, and often part of the head too. It protects the insect, like armor.

PUPATE
When an insect is changing from larva to adult, it is said to pupate. When it is a pupa, the insect is protected in a leathery case.

SAP
A sugary liquid that moves through the inside of a plant.

THORAX
The middle segment of an insect's body. Wings and legs are attached to the thorax.

TRANSPARENT
See-through.

TROPICAL
The areas that are found around the Equator, between the Tropic of Cancer and the Tropic of Capricorn. A tropical climate is usually very warm, with plenty of rain, all year round.

VENOM
A poison made in an animal's body and used to injure or kill another animal.

WINGSPAN
The measurement from one wing tip to another, across an animal's body.

INDEX

ACKNOWLEDGMENTS

Picture credits

(t=top, b=bottom, l=left, r=right, c=center, fc=front cover)

Alamy 12–13 blickwinkel, 52–53 imageBROKER

Nature PL 3tl Fabrice Cahez, 27br Visuals Unlimited, 27tl Visuals Unlimited, 31br Fabrice Cahez, 33bl Kim Taylor, 36bl Nature Production,

Science Photo Library 1b Eye of Science, 3tr Power and Syred, 4 Power and Syred, 6bl Frank Fox, 6tr David Aubrey, 8b Power and Syred, 8–9 Steve Gschmeissner, 9br Eye of Science, 9cr Steve Gschmeissner, 9tr Power and Syred, 10–11 Colin Varndell, 11br Colin Varndell, 11c Ian Gowland, 12br Clouds Hill Imaging Ltd, 13bl Alex Hyde, 13tr Natural History Museum, London, 14c Steve Gschmeissner, 16l Fabio Pupin/Visuals Unlimited, 17tl Steve Gschmeissner, 21tr Scott Camazine, 23br David Scharf, 24–25 Nicholas Reusens, 25tr Thierry Berrod, Mona Lisa Production, 26tr A Cosmos Blank, 26–27 Gilles Mermet, 28br Dr John Brackenbury, 28–29 Power and Syred, 29br Steve Gschmeissner, 29tr Power and Syred, 30cl Dr John Brackenbury, 31bl Dr Jeremy Burgess, 36–37 Steve Gschmeissner, 38tr F. Martinez Clavel, 39cr F. Martinez Clavel, 39tr Claude Nuridsany and Marie Perennou, 40cl Martin Shields, 41br Nicholas Reusens, 42bl Georgette Douwma, 43cr Natural History Museum, London, 44tl Eye of Science, 44–45 David Scharf, 45br Dr David Wheeler, 45tr David Scharf, 46–47 Philippe Psaila, 47br Thomas Shahan, 47tr Thomas Shahan, 48bl Steve Gschmeissner, 49br David Parker, 50br Larry West, 50–51 Dr Fred Hossler/Visuals Unlimited Inc, 51tr Martin Dohrn, 52tl Nigel Cattlin, 53tr Clouds Hill Imaging Ltd, 54cl Steve Percival, 54–55 Terry Priest/Visuals Unlimited Inc, 55bl Jeff Daly/Visuals, Unlimited Inc, 55cr Jeff Daly/Visuals Unlimited Inc, 55tr Steve Gschmeissner, 58bl Eye of Science, 58–59 Eye of Science, 59bl Nigel Cattlin, 59tl Fabio Pupin/Visuals Unlimited

Shutterstock 1tl irin-k, 1tr irin-k, 3bl Lightspring, 3 br smuay, 5 yanikap, 6–7 reptiles4all, 10bl Sanit Fuangnakhon, 11tr Erni, 12c irin-k, 14bc evantravels, 14br Eric Isselee, 14–15 Tyler Fox, 15br Katarina Christenson, 16br Awei, 16–17 Tomatito, 17br Henrik Larsson, 18br Ratchapol Yindeesuk, 18–19 Lakeview Images, 19br Eric Isselee, 19c Andrew Burgess, 19tl D. Kucharski K. Kucharska, 20c Eric Isselee, 20tr Cathy Keifer, 20–21 Greir, 22bl Preecha Ngamsrisan, 22–23 seeyou, 23cr smuay, 23tr natrot, 24bl Stanislav Fosenbauer, 25br Dr. Morley Read, 25tl skynetphoto, 28cl claffra, 30–31 Steve Byland, 31cr alexisvirid, 32br skynetphoto, 32–33 Lukas Hejtman, 33br MarkMirror, 33cr Lukas Hejtman, 34cl Kingfisher, 34cr Andrey Burmakin, 34–35 claffra, 35br Anton Kozyrev, 35tr Paul Looyen, 37bl David Lee, 37cr Chris Moody, 37tr Mauro Rodrigues, 38bl Seksan44, 38–39 Pukhouskaya Ina, 39br CreativeNature R.Zwerver, 40br Jiri Hodecek, 40–41 mrfiza, 41tr Henrik Larsson, 42bl Digoarpi, 42–43 alslutsky, 43br Sakdinon Kadchiangsaen, 46cr Pan Xunbin, 48–49 paulrommer, 49tr paulrommer, 50cl Kletr, 51br Thanapun, 53bl paulrommer, 53br alexsvirid, 56bl Tatsiana_S, 56cr Cristian Gusa, 56–57 Tatsiana_S, 57tr Cristian Gusa, 60 Eric Isselee, 62 Anton Kozyrev, 63 KOO